CW00832263

Carr

by Iain Gray

Lang**Syne**

PUBLISHING

WRITING *to* REMEMBER

79 Main Street, Newtongrange,
Midlothian EH22 4NA
Tel: 0131 344 0414   Fax: 0845 075 6085
E-mail: info@lang-syne.co.uk
www.langsyneshop.co.uk

Design by Dorothy Meikle
Printed by Ricoh Print Scotland
© Lang Syne Publishers Ltd 2012

ISBN 978-1-85217-463-7

Carmichael

MOTTO:
Always ready.

CREST:
An armoured hand
holding aloft a broken lance.

TERRITORY:
Lanarkshire, Galloway, Argyll.

NAME variations include:
Carmichail
Carmichale
Carmichan
Carmackhell
Mac Gillemichael *(Gaelic)*
Mac Michael *(Gaelic)*

The spirit of the clan means
much to thousands of people

Chapter one:

The origins of the clan system

by Rennie McOwan

The original Scottish clans of the Highlands and the great families of the Lowlands and Borders were gatherings of families, relatives, allies and neighbours for mutual protection against rivals or invaders.

Scotland experienced invasion from the Vikings, the Romans and English armies from the south. The Norman invasion of what is now England also had an influence on land-holding in Scotland. Some of these invaders stayed on and in time became 'Scottish'.

The word clan derives from the Gaelic language term 'clann', meaning children, and it was first used many centuries ago as communities were formed around tribal lands in glens and mountain fastnesses.

The format of clans changed over the centuries, but at its best the chief and his family held the land on behalf of all, like trustees, and the ordinary clansmen and women believed they had a blood relationship with the founder of their clan.

There were two way duties and obligations. An inadequate chief could be deposed and replaced by someone of greater ability.

Clan people had an immense pride in race. Their relationship with the chief was like adult children to a father and they had a real dignity.

The concept of clanship is very old and a more feudal notion of authority gradually crept in.

Pictland, for instance, was divided into seven principalities ruled by feudal leaders who were the strongest and most charismatic leaders of their particular groups.

By the sixth century the 'British' kingdoms of Strathclyde, Lothian and Celtic Dalriada (Argyll) had emerged and Scotland, as one nation, began to take shape in the time of King Kenneth MacAlpin.

Some chiefs claimed descent from ancient kings which may not have been accurate in every case.

By the twelfth and thirteenth centuries the clans and families were more strongly brought under the central control of Scottish monarchs.

Lands were awarded and administered more and more under royal favour, yet the power of the area clan chiefs was still very great.

The long wars to ensure Scotland's

independence against the expansionist ideas of English monarchs extended the influence of some clans and reduced the lands of others.

Those who supported Scotland's greatest king, Robert the Bruce, were awarded the territories of the families who had opposed his claim to the Scottish throne.

In the Scottish Borders country – the notorious Debatable Lands – the great families built up a ferocious reputation for providing warlike men accustomed to raiding into England and occasionally fighting one another.

Chiefs had the power to dispense justice and to confiscate lands and clan warfare produced a society where martial virtues – courage, hardiness, tenacity – were greatly admired.

Gradually the relationship between the clans and the Crown became strained as Scottish monarchs became more orientated to life in the Lowlands and, on occasion, towards England.

The Highland clans spoke a different language, Gaelic, whereas the language of Lowland Scotland and the court was Scots and in more modern times, English.

Highlanders dressed differently, had different

customs, and their wild mountain land sometimes seemed almost foreign to people living in the Lowlands.

It must be emphasised that Gaelic culture was very rich and story-telling, poetry, piping, the clarsach (harp) and other music all flourished and were greatly respected.

Highland culture was different from other parts of Scotland but it was not inferior or less sophisticated.

Central Government, whether in London or Edinburgh, sometimes saw the Gaelic clans as a challenge to their authority and some sent expeditions into the Highlands and west to crush the power of the Lords of the Isles.

Nevertheless, when the eighteenth century Jacobite Risings came along the cause of the Stuarts was mainly supported by Highland clans.

The word Jacobite comes from the Latin for James – Jacobus. The Jacobites wanted to restore the exiled Stuarts to the throne of Britain.

The monarchies of Scotland and England became one in 1603 when King James VI of Scotland (1st of England) gained the English throne after Queen Elizabeth died.

The Union of Parliaments of Scotland and England, the Treaty of Union, took place in 1707.

Some Highland clans, of course, and Lowland families opposed the Jacobites and supported the incoming Hanoverians.

After the Jacobite cause finally went down at Culloden in 1746 a kind of ethnic cleansing took place. The power of the chiefs was curtailed. Tartan and the pipes were banned in law.

Many emigrated, some because they wanted to, some because they were evicted by force. In addition, many Highlanders left for the cities of the south to seek work.

Many of the clan lands became home to sheep and deer shooting estates.

But the warlike traditions of the clans and the great Lowland and Border families lived on, with their descendants fighting bravely for freedom in two world wars.

Remember the men from whence you came, says the Gaelic proverb, and to that could be added the role of many heroic women.

The spirit of the clan, of having roots, whether Highland or Lowland, means much to thousands of people.

*Clan warfare produced a society where courage
and tenacity were greatly admired*

Chapter two:

On the field of battle

Found in a number of rather bewildering spelling variations that include Carmichail and Carmichale, Carmichael is a surname that has resonated throughout the pages of Scottish history from earliest times.

A name meaning 'son of Michael' or 'servant of Michael' it also has a separate derivation from the village of Carmichael, between Biggar and Lanark, in present day South Lanarkshire, in the Scottish Lowlands.

A clan quite distinct from Clan Carmichael of Lanarkshire was also present from earliest times in Galloway, in the southwest of Scotland, and further northwest in the Highlands of Argyll.

The Gaelic form of the name for this family was *Mac Gillemichael*, or *Mac Michael*, and it was the Mac Michaels of Argyll who are recognised as a sept, or sub-branch, of the proud West Highland clan the Stewarts of Appin.

It is through these separate identifications with Clan Carmichael of Lanarkshire and the Stewarts of Appin that bearers of the name today can lay claim to a proud heritage rooted deep in the ancient soil of Scotland.

In Lanarkshire, the Carmichaels were closely allied with Clan Douglas, and it was this powerful clan that in the late fourteenth century granted the lands of Carmichael to Sir John Carmichael.

Also known as the barony of Carmichael, these lands were in turn originally granted to Clan Douglas by the great warrior king Robert the Bruce in 1321.

Recognised as 30th Chief of the Name and Arms of Carmichael and 26th Baron of the lands of Carmichael, Richard Carmichael and his family, as proud custodians of the family heritage, today operate a working farm and the Discover Carmichael Centre on the ancient baronial lands.

It was as a close ally of Clan Douglas, whose motto is *Never Behind* and crest a green salamander, that the Carmichaels fought at the battle of Otterburn in August of 1388.

James Douglas, 2nd Earl of Douglas, had led a Scottish force over the border into Northumberland and ravaged the countryside around Newcastle and Durham.

Henry Percy, 1st Earl of Northumberland, had

despatched his two sons, Ralph Percy and Henry "Hotspur" Percy to engage with the Scots near Otterburn – while he lay in wait at Alnwick to cut off what he confidently and mistakenly thought would later be the Scots' disorganised retreat back over the border.

But the battle resulted in a resounding defeat for the English – although Douglas himself was killed.

So significant was the Scottish victory, one in which the Carmichaels had participated, that it later became the subject of two popular ballads – including *The Ballad of Chevy Chase* and *The Battle of Otterburn*.

An odd footnote to the battle comes from nearly 600 years later, in 1960, when a number of witnesses claimed they had seen a 'phantom army' near the site of the battle.

One of the witnesses, who had been travelling in a taxi on the road running past the battlefield, said: "Suddenly the engine died, the fare-meter went haywire and the taxi felt as if it was being forced against an invisible wall.

"The soldiers seemed to close in on us and then fade into thin air."

There were also reports that the 'phantom army' had been witnessed at other times in the past.

On decidedly more solid ground than 'phantom' armies, Sir John Carmichael of Douglasdale gained fame as a member of the Franco-Scots army at the battle of Baugé.

Fought in March of 1421 at Baugé, east of the French town of Angers during the Hundred Years War, the battle resulted in a major victory for the Franco-Scots over an English army led by Thomas of Lancaster, 1st Duke of Clarence, brother of England's Henry IV.

The Franco-Scots, who fought under the terms of the famed 'Auld Alliance' between the two nations, were commanded by Gilbert de Lafayette, the Constable of France, and John Stewart, 2nd Earl of Buchan.

Among the 6,000 Scots on the battlefield was Sir John Carmichael, who gained glory after charging the Duke of Clarence and unseating him from his horse – breaking his lance in the process – while the Duke was later slain by other Scots as he lay on the ground.

It was in commemoration of his deed that the Carmichaels later proudly adopted the crest on their Coat of Arms of an armoured hand holding aloft a broken lance.

In recognition of his services to the French cause, Carmichael was rewarded with the lucrative Bishopric of Orleans and became known in France as Jean de St Michel.

Hosted by Richard Carmichael, 30th Chief of Carmichael, an International Carmichael Gathering was held on their ancient lands in the summer of 2010 – with one of its themes a celebration of the life and times of one of its famous female forebears.

This was Kathleen Carmichael, a daughter of Sir John Carmichael of the Meadowflats, Lanarkshire, cadet branch of the clan, who was a favoured mistress of James V, who reigned from 1513 to 1542.

The son of their union, James Stewart, whose birth was legitimised by Papal decree, became Prior of Coldingham Abbey.

A half-brother of the ill-starred Mary, Queen of Scots, his son was Francis Stewart, Earl of Bothwell.

In May of 1546, four years after the death of James V and during the troubled minority of his heir Mary, Peter Carmichael of the Balmedie, Fifeshire, branch of the family was one of the murderers of Cardinal Beaton.

Appointed Archbishop of St Andrews in 1539

and made Papal legate to Scotland five years later, the powerful Cardinal incurred the wrath of many when, in March of 1546 he was instrumental in the arrest, trial and subsequent execution by burning of the popular nonconformist preacher George Wishart.

It was in revenge for this that a party of powerful conspirators, who included Carmichael and William Kirkcaldy of Grange, murdered him after gaining entry to his private chambers in the castle of St Andrews.

Not satisfied with merely murdering him, they then mutilated his corpse and hanged it from a castle window for all to see.

As punishment, Carmichael was sentenced to spend time fettered to an oar in the galleys – a fate also shared by the Protestant Reformer John Knox.

In common with Knox, however, the rapidly shifting religious and political allegiances of the times soon found him released from his grim fate.

Chapter three:

Rebellion and anarchy

It was in the particularly turbulent sixteenth century that Sir John Carmichael held a powerful position as one of the Wardens of the Borders Marches – with the onerous remit of attempting to control the anarchic activities of the Border Reivers.

These reivers took their name from their lawless custom of reiving, or raiding, not only their neighbours' livestock, but also that of their neighbours across the border.

The word 'bereaved', for example, indicating to have suffered loss, derives from the original 'reived', meaning to have suffered loss of property.

A Privy Council report graphically described how the "wild incests, adulteries, convocation of the lieges, shooting and wearing of hackbuts, pistols, lances, daily bloodshed, oppression, and disobedience in civil matters, neither are nor has been punished."

A constant thorn in the flesh of both the English and Scottish authorities was the cross-border raiding and pillaging carried out by well-mounted and heavily armed men, the contingent from the Scottish side of the border known and feared as 'moss troopers.'

In an attempt to bring order to what was known as the wild 'debateable land' on both sides of the border, Alexander II of Scotland had in 1237 signed the Treaty of York, which for the first time established the Scottish border with England as a line running from the Solway to the Tweed.

On either side of the border there were three 'marches' or areas of administration, the West, East and Middle Marches, and a warden governed these.

Sir John Carmichael, known as the Keeper of Liddesdale, was Warden of the West March.

Complaints from either side of the border were dealt with on Truce Days, when the wardens of the different marches would act as arbitrators.

There was also a law known as the Hot Trod, that granted anyone who had their livestock stolen the right to pursue the thieves and recover their property.

In the Scottish borderlands, the Homes and Swintons dominated the East March, while the Armstrongs, Maxwells, Johnstones and Grahams were pre-eminent in Sir John's territory of the West March.

The Kerrs, along with the Douglases and Elliots, held sway in the Middle March.

What occasionally united the warring factions was opposition to their counterparts across the border, and in July of 1575 Sir John Carmichael led a party of his countrymen in what became celebrated in ballad as the *Raid of the Redeswire*.

One of the last such Border raids of its kind, it took place at the Cheviot Pass, when the heavily-armed Scots met with an equally heavily-armed body of English – ostensibly to discuss the terms of a truce.

Insults were traded by both sides before this gave way to full-scale battle and the eventual routing of the English and the death of several of their leaders, including Sir George Heron, Keeper of Redesdale.

The Union of the Crowns of Scotland and England did not occur until the accession of James I (James VI of Scotland) to the English throne in 1603 – and the Raid of the Redeswire is recognised as the last major battle between the Kingdom of Scotland and the Kingdom of England.

Five years later, Sir John Carmichael was ambushed and murdered by a party of Armstrongs as he was en route to attend a Warden Court.

Moving from the Clan Carmichael home of Lanarkshire, in the Lowlands, to the West Highlands, bearers of the Carmichael name in its Gaelic versions

of Mac Gillemichael and Mac Michael were kinsfolk
of the Stewarts of Appin.

It was through this close kinship that they
are recognised, along with others who include the
Livingstones and Mackinlays, as a sept of the clan.

As such, they shared in both the clan's
glorious fortunes and tragic misfortunes.

Known as the Loyal Clan because of their
staunch support of the Royal House of Stewart (or
Stuart), the motto of the clan is *Wither will ye* and crest
the head of a unicorn.

With their main seat from earliest times being
Castle Stalker, in Appin, in the north of Argyll, they
were frequently to be found on the field of battle in the
Stuart cause – along with their Carmichael kinsfolk.

A bitter civil war raged in Scotland from 1638
to 1649 between the forces of those Presbyterian Scots
who had signed a National Covenant that opposed the
divine right of the Stuart monarchy and Royalists such
as James Graham, 1st Marquis of Montrose, whose
prime allegiance was to Charles I.

Although Montrose had initially supported
the Covenant, his conscience later forced him to
switch sides, and it was at his side that the Stewarts of
Appin and kinsfolk such as the Carmichaels fought.

His great campaigns were fought from 1644 to 1645 – a year that became known as the Year of Miracles because of his brilliant military successes.

These included the battle of Inverlochy, in February of 1645, when the Earl of Argyll was forced to ignominiously flee in his galley after 1,500 of his Covenanters were wiped out in a surprise attack.

What makes Montrose's victory all the more notable is that his hardy forces had arrived at Inverlochy after an exhausting 36-hour march south through knee-deep snow from the area of the present-day Fort Augustus.

He enjoyed another great victory at Kilsyth in August of the same year, but final defeat came at the battle of Philiphaugh, near Selkirk, less than a month later.

The Stewarts of Appin and their Mac Michael/Carmichael kinsfolk were also prominent in their support of Prince Charles Edward Stuart.

The prince had landed on the small Outer Hebridean island of Eriskay on July 22, 1745, arriving on the mainland at Loch nan Uamh three days later.

The Stuart Standard was raised a few weeks later, on August 19, at Glenfinnan, on Loch Shiel, and the Stewarts of Appin were among those clans who rallied to what is known as the Jacobite cause.

Victory was achieved at the battle of Prestonpans in September, and in October the confident prince and his army set off on the long march south to London to claim what was believed to be the rightful Stuart inheritance of the throne.

The army reached only as far as Derby, however, before the controversial decision was taken in early December to withdraw back over the border.

Jacobite hopes were finally dashed forever at the battle of Culloden, fought on Drummossie Moor, near Inverness, on April 16, 1746.

Hundreds of clansmen died on the battlefield while hundreds of others, including Carmichaels, died later from their wounds and the brutal treatment of their Government captors.

From the bloody battlefield of Culloden and back to the Carmichaels of Lanarkshire, Sir James Carmichael had been raised to the peerage in 1647 as 1st Lord Carmichael, while his son married a Douglas heir.

Their son, in turn, was created Earl of Hyndford as reward for his support of the Royalist cause of Charles I.

The 2nd Earl of Hyndford, however, supported the Parliamentary cause and helped to defeat Montrose's forces at the battle of Philiphaugh.

In keeping with what is frequently the complex genealogy of noble Scottish families and clans such as the Carmichaels, it was through marriage, in this case the marriage of Lady Margaret Carmichael, a daughter of the 2nd Earl of Hyndford, to Sir John Anstruther, that the family eventually became, in 1817, known as Carmichael-Anstruther.

Nearly 165 years later, in 1981, following the death a year earlier of Sir Windham Carmichael-Anstruther, 25th Baron of Carmichael, Richard Carmichael – then a young accountant living and working in New Zealand – was officially recognised as 26th Baron of Carmichael and 30th Chief of the Name.

The family name then reverted back from Carmichael-Anstruther to Carmichael – returning to its roots in more ways than one as the 30th Chief and his family settled on the ancient Carmichael lands.

Chapter four:

On the world stage

Born in 1920 in Hull, Yorkshire, the son of an optician, Ian Carmichael was the English actor of stage, film and television whose acting career was interrupted by the Second World War, when he served with the Royal Armoured Corps, reaching the rank of major.

Films in which he appeared include the 1954 *Betrayed*, which starred Lana Turner and Clark Gable, and, a year later *The Colditz Story*.

He is best known, however, for his comedic roles in a number of films that include *Private's Progress*, *I'm All Right, Jack*, the 1966 *School for Scandal* and the 1971 *The Magnificent Seven Deadly Sins*.

Television roles during the 1960s and 1970s included that of Bertie Wooster in *The World of Jeeves* while, before his death in 2010, by which time he had been awarded an MBE, *Heartbeat* and *The Royal*.

In contemporary acting, **Laury Carmichael**, born in 1986, is the British actress known for her role in the popular *Downton Abbey* television series as

Lady Edith Crawley, while film credits include the 2011 *Tinker Tailor Soldier Spy*.

From the stage to the world of music, **Hoagy Carmichael** was the legendary American composer, pianist, singer and actor who was born Howard Hoagland Carmichael in 1899 in Bloomington, Indiana.

Of Scottish ancestry through his father, Howard Clyde Carmichael, his parents gave him the middle name 'Hoagland' in recognition of a circus troupe called The Hoaglands who had lodged for a brief time with them while his mother, Lida, was pregnant with him.

His father was a horse-drawn taxi driver, and Hoagy appears to have inherited his musical talent from his mother, an accomplished pianist who provided musical accompaniment for silent movies.

Learning to play piano, Carmichael earned money by playing at dances and parties while studying for, and later obtaining, a law degree from Indiana University.

By 1926, he had met and become friendly with the great jazz coronetist Bix Beiderbecke and later with Louis Armstrong.

His musical skills were fully honed by 1928,

when he wrote his first major hit, *Stardust*, followed by others that include *Rockin' Chair*, his 1930 *Georgia on My Mind* and the 1951 *My Resistance is Low*.

In 1960, the Ray Charles version of *Georgia on My Mind* became a major hit, receiving Grammy Awards for Best Male Vocal and Best Popular Single and later adopted as the official song of the State of Georgia.

Carmichael also appeared in films that include 1946's *The Best Years of Our Lives* and the 1952 *The Las Vegas Story*.

Author of two books of autobiography, *The Stardust Road* and *Sometimes I Wonder*, he died in 1981.

An inductee of the Gennett Records Walk of Fame in Richmond, Indiana, he is also honoured through the Hoagy Carmichael Landmark Sculpture at Indiana University.

Born in 1953, **Greg Carmichael** is the guitarist who has been a member since 1985 of the contemporary British jazz group Acoustic Alchemy, whose major hits include *Red Dust and Spanish Lace*.

Also in contemporary music, **Jesse Carmichael**, born in 1979 in Boulder, Colorado, is the American musician who plays keyboards for the band Maroon 5.

Back in time and to the Carmichael homeland of Scotland, **Alexander Carmichael**, born in 1832 at Taylochan, on the island of Lismore, was the folklorist responsible for the multi-volume *Carmina Gadelica – The Hymns of the Gael*.

Documenting throughout his lifetime the traditions of the Gaelic Highlanders, he also contributed to John Francis Campbell's noted *The Popular Tales of the West Highlands*; he died in 1912.

On the field of battle, **John Carmichael**, born in 1893 in Glenmavis, Lanarkshire was a Scottish recipient of the Victoria Cross (VC), the highest award for gallantry in the face of enemy action for British and Commonwealth forces.

He had been a sergeant in the 9th Battalion, The North Staffordshire Regiment (The Prince of Wales's) during the First World War, when in September of 1917 near Hill 60, Zwartelen, Belgium, he performed the deed for which he won the VC.

It was while excavating a trench that he spotted a grenade whose fuse had started to burn. Ordering his men to get clear, he put his steel helmet over the grenade and then stood on the helmet.

The grenade exploded, blowing him out of the trench and seriously injuring him; had he opted instead to throw the grenade out of the trench, he knew it would have endangered others.

His VC is now on display at the Staffordshire Regimental Museum in Lichfield.

Also during the First World War, **Sir James Carmichael**, born in 1868 and who died in 1934, was the British Army officer who served for a time as director of materials at the Ministry of Munitions.

In the creative world of art, **Franklin Carmichael**, born in 1890 in Orilla, Ontario, was the Canadian artist who, after studying at the Ontario School of Art in Toronto, founded the Ontario Society of Painters in Watercolours, and, in 1933, the Canadian Group of Painters – also known as the Group of Seven.

A teacher at Ontario College of Art from 1932 until his death in 1945, he was also renowned for his landscapes of Ontario.

Bearers of the Carmichael name have also been prominent in the often cut-throat world of politics.

Born on the Scottish island of Islay in 1965, **Alistair Carmichael** is the Liberal Democrat politician who has been Member of Parliament (MP) for the seat of Orkney and Shetland since 2001.

A solicitor and former Procurator Fiscal

Depute, he has also served as Liberal Democrat spokesman for Scotland and Northern Ireland and as Deputy Chief Whip in the Liberal Democrat-Conservative coalition government.

Born in Glasgow in 1894, **James Carmichael** was the Scottish Labour politician whose father, George Carmichael, was one of the founding members of the Independent Labour Party (ILP).

Serving in the the former Glasgow Corporation from 1939 to 1946, he later served as MP for Glasgow Bridgeton; retiring as an MP in 1961, he died five years later.

He was the father of Neil Carmichael, **Baron Carmichael of Kelvingrove**, the Labour Party politician who was born in Glasgow in 1921.

In common with his father, he served for a time on Glasgow Town Council, before being elected in 1962 as MP for the former Glasgow seat of Glasgow Woodside.

Awarded a life peerage in 1983 and serving for a time in the House of Lords as Labour's spokesman on transport and Scotland, he died in 2001.

Not only a politician but also a prominent Nova Scotia businessman, **James Carmichael** was born in 1819 in New Glasgow, Nova Scotia.

Representing Pictou in the Canadian House of Commons as an anti-Confederate, then as a Liberal, from 1867 to 1872 and from 1874 to 1878, he also represented Nova Scotia in the Canadian Senate from 1898 to 1903.

He became the owner of his father's retail and shipping business during the 1850s, and later pioneered the building and use of iron and steel ships in Nova Scotia; he died in 1903.

Born in 1941 in Port of Spain, Trinidad and Tobago, but moving to Harlem, New York, at the age of 11, **Stokely Carmichael** was the black activist who was closely involved with the 'Black Power' movement in the United States through the Black Panther Party; he died in 1998.

Bearers of the Carmichael name have excelled, and continue to excel, in the competitive world of sport.

Born in 1961 in Miami, Florida, **Chris Carmichael** is the retired professional cyclist who, in 1986, was a member of the first U.S. cycling team to compete in the Tour de France.

In American football, **Harold Carmichael**, born in 1949 in Jacksonville, Florida, is the former wide receiver who played for teams that include the

Philadelphia Eagles and the Dallas Cowboys.

Born in 1965 in Steamboat Springs, Colorado, **Nelson Carmichael** is the American freestyle skier who won a bronze medal at the 1992 Winter Olympics.

In the rough and tumble that is the game of rugby, **Sandy Carmichael** is the former tight-head prop forward who was born in Glasgow in 1944 and who earned 50 caps from 1967 to 1978 with the Scotland national rugby union team.

In the highly cerebral realms of mathematics, **Robert D. Carmichael**, born in 1879 in Goodwater, Alabama, and who died in 1967, was the leading American mathematician famed for his discovery of what have become known as Carmichael Numbers – relating to the complex properties of prime numbers.

In the equally cerebral realms of philosophy, **Gershom Carmichael**, born in London in 1672 and of Scottish parentage, is recognised today as 'the real founder of the Scottish school of philosophy'.

Educated at St Andrews University, where he also held a teaching post for a number of years, he was appointed to Glasgow University in 1694, later serving as professor of moral philosophy from 1727 until his death two years later.

One particularly selfless bearer of the Carmichael name was the Northern Irish missionary **Amy Wilson Carmichael**, born in 1867 in Millisle, Co. Down.

It was through the Presbyterian Church Missionary Society that in 1896 she founded a mission in Dohnavur, India, remaining there until her death 55 years later – having written detailed accounts of her missionary work and an anthology of verse, *Mountain Breezes*.